IN THE SKIN HOUSE

In the Skin House

£1·99

A

JENI COUZYN

BLOODAXE BOOKS

ISBN: 1 85224 254 X

First published 1993 by
Bloodaxe Books Ltd,
P.O. Box 1SN,
Newcastle upon Tyne NE99 1SN.

Bloodaxe Books Ltd acknowledges
the financial assistance of Northern Arts.

Llewellyn Vaughan-Lee is the author of a number of books
on Sufism, dreamwork, and Jungian Psychology.

Cover printing by J. Thomson Colour Printers Ltd, Glasgow.

Printed in Great Britain by
Cromwell Press Ltd, Broughton Gifford, Melksham, Wiltshire.

FOREWORD

There is nothing more intimate than our own inner journey, opening to our own mystery. Within us we contain a universe of dreams and longings, hidden secrets waiting to be unveiled. For each of us this inner opening is unique. It is our own most personal wonder, our own most precious dream. Yet there are themes that speak to us all, that echo and activate our own dreams, make more real our own mystery.

In the Skin House is Jeni Couzyn's own inner story. Her poems speak with the truth of someone who has walked the dangerous borderland that connects the two worlds. Her images speak of the fire and the burning, of the tenderness and the flowering that take us beyond the known world of familiar forms. She takes us into the naked and barren landscape of a wayfarer searching for her own truth, discovering how she is both the puppet and the puppeteer and has to confront the strange contradictions of being human.

She begins with a poem about dreaming and waking. Do we just dream we are awake or is there a real awakening from this stuff of dreams that we are made of? In a story by the Chinese philosopher Chang Tzu a man dreams that he is a butterfly, flying happily about. Then he awakens from this dream only to wonder if he is a man who has dreamt he was a butterfly, or actually a butterfly dreaming that he is a man. This is the paradoxical landscape that is home to the dreamer, the poet and the mystic. Jeni embraces all these elements as she images her own searching, her desire to break the patterns of appearances and discover what her own skin house really contains.

Her poems draw back veils, revealing both the texture of her dreams and also mirrors in which the reader senses himself. She

5

beckons us inward and helps to illuminate our own intimate self. There is the danger of this revelation, this 'shimmering flame under the skin', but more than that there is the tenderness of love speaking to itself. Because underneath the harshness of her drive to be truthful is woven the theme of love, and with it the sense of love's mystery in which the dream is more real than any tangible truth.

These poems evoke no sense of any outer lover; the real love affair takes place upon an inner stage. Her lover is within her 'always' because this is the inner essence of any love affair: the magic that we search for in outer relationships, the ecstasy that we experience in love-making, is born from an inner union, what the alchemists called the *mysterium coniunctionis*. The great mystical poet Rumi expresses this when he says:

> The minute I heard my first love story
> I started looking for you, not knowing
> how blind that was.
> Lovers don't finally meet somewhere.
> They're in each other all along.

This is the love affair that unfolds *In the Skin House*. She wonders 'Have I invented you?' Yet all her work, the honesty and self-exploration, is but a preparation for this inner meeting.

Sometimes her lover appears as a man whose song in her body makes her young, sometimes as an angel inside her calling her to surrender into love. Sometimes the lover seems present, sometimes there is no one there. But amidst her images of opening and flowering is the definite statement that '*A bud cannot be opened / by a man*'. The invisible lover is the one whose embrace her whole being craves.

Jeni's mysticism is neither abstract nor ascetic, but belongs to the school of lovers like Mary Magdalene. Mary was the first to see the risen Christ, and that vision is the promise of a love which is not limited – it awakens us to another reality. Jeni makes this passion real. She does not deny the body, but embraces it and goes beyond its boundaries. She is a woman in the arms of her inner lover, surrendering to the mystery of the soul. Telling her own story she offers a mirror for others in which they can see and taste this dimension of their own longing, feel the need to unite the two worlds within themselves.

for my teacher

1

He Enters the Dream

I dreamed I was asleep
and one woke me.
Each atom separate and on fire
I walked among the sleepers:
Awake! Awake!
Then in the dream I perceived
that being awake
was part of the dream
and dreamed I truly woke.
Thus in the dream
I wake and wake
and cannot wake.

He is a jailbird
this tall one
with spread wings
offering the grail.
His crime
abusing his daughter –
his grime.
She in the white skirts
and frail cage of bone.

The cold, cold well
at the world's end
your love.
A sieve – the stepmother's gift –
my heart.

We swimmers
in a churning river –
those who are drowned
are swept to the ocean,
those who are not drowned
are swept to the ocean.
Upstream, downstream
it makes no difference.

The meadow we grew green in
flickers on, off.
The watchers without eyes
call us without words
have thrown a current
like a net, feather-light
across the water.
I think it is music.

We must be dust-mote,
bird-bone.

All night the snow-beasts
rampaged through my house.
I thought it was stone
but it was matchwood.
I thought I was a queen
but I am a beggar-woman.
I want a place to be with you
where no one has been.

The bombs are in the sky now.
All the people are wailing –
no no no no!
Yet the lambs tip themselves
dangerously onto their feet
delighted – yes to the snow
bitter hills, green wind.

So you're back.
Listen to this life splinter
clish clish
like blown glass
like snow-crystals
icon after icon.

Do not move, not a twitch
not a nerve.
I am cut loose from the tug-ship
that dragged me from the harbour.
There it goes, tooting and puffing smoke
back where it came from.
The ocean is black, huge
empty in all directions.

Time to attend to drains:
Dead smell and a pool of rotting.
Time to attend to chimneys:
This has been on fire, this has burned
rightly.
Time to attend the outhouse.
Time to attend the inhouse.

The puppet is frightened.
It wants to be liked.
It wants to be thought pretty.
It wants to be thought clever.
I give it nothing.
Ayee, it whines,
Put me back in my box
close the lid.
The puppet must give up wanting
this and that.
It must be empty
so I can slip my hand into
its little velvet spaces
and move those papier mâché lips
cold eyes, useless hands.

Death, you are tramping about in my body
like a man in a black leather jacket
with a vicious dog only just under control.
Please go home.
Have a bath.
Light a candle.
Light your bloodhound in its kennel.
Lie down on your bed with a damp cloth
over your eyes.
Now think my name.
See how quietly I come.

Web, intricate in air.
Time, spider at its centre.
Friends here we are
knee-deep in silk.
Tiptoeing will not help us,
pirouetting and bowing to each other.
Yet why do I look around
as if some giant hand
could sweep away this story?

Each mandala of lives
has a single life
at its centre.
Can I bespeak
this flurry of snow-grains,
palace of crystals?

Autumn. Precious metal in my veins.
Taste of death in my mouth.
How could I speak of the chestnut?
It is on fire within my body.

It is not that you enter.
You were here always
under the eyelids
under the skin
under the endless busybody
rushing of the blood.
It is not that I enter you.
I was in you always
but briefly,
from the caul of sleep
I quicken.

2

He Illuminates the Stone

1

The puppet is made in my body.
The angel of death-in-life
is present during the making.
The puppet is a network of wires
fine as spider thread,
and patterns of threaded cells
like tapestries of coloured beads
intricately webbed
each in the right order.
The angel with exquisite hands
is weaving the puppet
within my body, running current
through the fine wires, joining
the hair-like tapestries of cells
each to its own live terminal.

I feel the presence of the angel
growing within me, yet travelling towards me
as if from the outer reaches
of the stars.
The stranger within my body
is the size of a pin head
pipes my mind
but the feeling within me
that feels the presence
speaks from a different knowledge:
Within my body I am vast.
The angel within me
travelling towards me from the cosmos
has brought the cosmos
into my body.

What is it, who is it
travelling towards you?
I feel it as love.
But what is it, this love feeling?
Time is soon to answer this with words.

2

I am clinging to the strings of the world
pulled this way and that.
Surrender, says the angel,
striking my knuckles with sharp pain.
I ache in my spine
and behind my eyes.
I am sick in the pit of my stomach.
The pain is in my pride and in my wanting.
Surrender, thunders the angel
within my body.
It is threading new cells
into a structure like a cathedral
and I protesting
This is my body, mine.
I cannot see you.
I don't understand what you are doing.
Surrender, sighs the angel
a sea of sweetness that enfolds me.
Love. Surrender.

3

The puppet is born of my body.
Now death is the lantern
behind the skin
that shows it transparent.
It is the light within the stone
revealing star spaces
between the molecules.
Enter.
Miles to go from atom to atom
electron to nucleus.
In Death Country I walk easy
through the solid substances,
death within me I go lightly clad.
Between the fierce particles of the sun
a darker brilliance
illuminates the earth.
The angel of death-in-life
is born of my body.

3

He is Heard in the Wind

I have many pairs of eyes.
One is for celebrating gardens
One is for rooting out dirt in corners
One is for mining into the future
One is for treasure-hunting into the past.
One pair of eyes is for breaking you into little pieces
One is for putting you together again new
One is for dressing you in a white robe
One is for drinking holy communion
from the bowl of your breath.

Lips, speak only his word.
Breath, be his bird.
Eyes, his glance.
Body, his dance.

Charm faltered in your light.
Beneath it
blank eyes of the android
machine
seeking to perpetuate itself.
Love,
harsh, critical, ceaseless
I cannot deny you.
The heaving and whimpering
of the little body
has nothing to do with it.

I am hu – the empty
you are man.
I am wo
you are within me.
You creep from my body
into your life
like a pale mosquito.

Within the skin house
I contain you.
As if strangers
in twin beds
in an attic spareroom
one lying wakeful
afloat in the dark.
Bodies inches apart
stretch out a hand
and no one is there.

Have I invented you?
Out there, an electric impulse
that has touched a growing point in me,
out there, no one?
I hold my stillness
pressed to your point of entry
like a flame.
The current pulses through me.
It rises from the earth like sap.
I think of those
growing up from the root
or those impaled.

Death.
How else to reach me
through the thicknesses?
One more roof gone.
The house a temple.

The blackness is glass
will not let me pass.
Is it thee beneath
calling this way, through!
I hurl myself against it
purpled with bruises
bones all broken.
This way, through!

Then I perceived that house
garden
rows of ancestors
leatherbound books and
paintings of angels
belonged to you.
Even the child
was your daughter.
I was nothing – less than nothing
a housekeeper who had utterly
forgotten myself.

All my work now is
restoration.
The insides of buds.
Thought within the word.
Little messes of toxins
within the blood.

Wanting for myself
is useless to the world –
vagabond bones.
Wanting from the world –
gangster gold
useless to me.
Let me be field
empty of crop
with poppy for blood –
Your footprint
as you pass.

You entered the muscles with a paring knife
like a strong old woman
peeling potatoes.
You entered the veins with a wire brush.
Because I have prepared for you all year
clearing the builder's rubble
from what I called
my house –
welcome.

4

He Enters a Man

A man passes in the street.
His shoes are a kind we make
in my native village.
Is it the shoes I know him by,
or the eyes? or the song?
I know his shirt of flame,
which loom, which skein,
who spun his skin,
who ravelled his hurt.
He sings of my home. Snowflakes
pause in their fall.
Birds become stone.

Where are you?
I am suffused with
a colour. Orchid.
It is not in time
this colour
this wonder.
The I squats in time
a frog glaring
at its reflection.
I moving dust
from one place
to another.

How shall I know you when we meet?

You will open your mouth to speak,
words will become birds and fly
directly to heaven
but that is not the sign.

Your voice will run over me like honey
enter through the pores of my skin
till each cell opens
a sweet-centred flower
but that is not the sign.

Nor is the drum-beat
at the source of the waterfall,
nor the flame
at the source of the drum-beat.

I gave you my love
you sold it for bread.
Now I have ten thousand hearts
all clamouring:
'Eat *me*, eat *me*!'

You have drawn my love
like a white doe out of the thicket.
You wear me like a jewel in your forehead.
You set me like an oil lamp in your window.
How precarious
these transformations!
When the magic is completed
you will have to nail me to your wall
as a trophy.

Your song in my body
is making me young.
I remember that the flesh
grows and dies to God's breath
which transcends
the law of earth.
Your song works in my body
not in time
but in the moment
as I see your love
in my mirror.

If I turn aside
it will flow back into the earth
a dark patch of blood.
I hold it precious, cradled on my breath –
bud, heavy as a butcher's heart –
spotted lotus flaring from swamps –
blood-flower, passion flower
moonflower of dark air.
It stirs on each breath I take
heavy, hidden.

I wait for you
like a crazy person.
Someone offers me money.
Someone asks for money.
The wasps cover my hands
and my eyes.
They enter my mouth and my lungs.
They call it
'reality'.

I've released my song
on the fronds of my mind.

Now my heart puts on its showshoes
and begins to trudge after, slowly
and with blind faith.
Snow-blind in a white landscape
I don't know the direction.

I face the white waste.
I paddle out over the snow
awkward in my snowshoes.
If you are death it doesn't matter
which way I go.
You're all around me
within each snowflake, each atom
illuminating everything.

If you're life, beloved,
the case is the same.
Whichever direction I take
will bring me to you.
But how to reach you
across the distances?

I think of you, snug in your hut
or perhaps
half-buried in a snowdrift
knowing I will come
not knowing who I am, or how, or why
but the certainty of miracles.

One Mary walks beside you
brings you food and dries
your feet with her hair.

One Mary covers the broken
body with her cloak.

One Mary pushes the stone
from the entrance to the garden.

When you leave me at the station
my hands are empty.
I lay them at your feet
like gloves of fine leather.
I take nothing with me that is yours.
I take nothing with me that is mine.

You speak
from within the rose,
your colour velvet:
Put away your hands.
A bud cannot be opened
by a man.

A man carries me across the water
into his boat as if I were a child,
shows me his lobster pots,
shows me seals in their cave
under the cliffs.
A stranger takes me in his boat.
Your face is everywhere I look.

5

He is Heard in the Heart

The deepest shadows cast
the brightest angels.
Last first, worst best.
Satan in his flight
through blackness
Lord of Light.

Heart, make the shepherd's leap
when you feel his lash
bound over the skies
when you burn with pain
your cries in this desert
rise like rain
upwards from the ground.

Cool my pain!
Lift me from the fire!
I search for you everywhere
hoarse with grief
suddenly hear you:
I am the fire.
I am your prayer.

Empty your heart.
And when it is empty
let your enemy cut it out.
And when he has taken
each scarlet shred
give him your husk of ribbed bone.
Give him your arms and legs and eyes,
seeds in the shed,
cymbals in the attic –
Let him take it all.
Even the pearl
drowning in your throat.

You think of your heart
as a big basin, overflowing
and you're in a panic.
You're afraid of drowning
in your own body.
This image has led you
into confusion.
Think of your heart as a doorway.
Let the hordes march through you.

Empty your hands.
Such clever fingers,
ten thousand monkeys.
You think they are for holding –
try using them for letting go.
Hold a flame in your hand –
pain.
Be the flame.
Become a bonfire at midnight
on an empty beach
each star attentive.

You say you have not seen him
with your eyes.
The seed also is blind
yet rises to sun.
If it had eyes, as you do
it might calculate, consider,
mistake, as you do
full moon on a winter night.

You accuse the other
and defend yourself.
Try another way.
Become an eagle on the moor.
Become a mouse in the heather.
Be eagle and mouse at the same
time, and then become
the moor itself,
scent of the heather.
Knowing yourself,
release the other.

Still you are raising
your lamentation.
A ruined castle
walls so thick your arms
barely span them.
Eyelash on life's collar,
an outbreath completed.

Light that lies softly
without bruising the dark
each particle a pearl
in its velvet pod;
Music, the notes slipping
silent as vivid fish;
Stillness, an endless
streaming from the source –
Your presence.

How shall I leave your house?
If I choose the gravel that loops
cautiously to the gate
I'll find myself in water
body jerked under.

Or I may choose the rockery
that rears at the back.
Launching into a vertical
I'm trapped between overhang and drop
can't climb
daren't look down.

Why must I go?
Fling my life out of the door
and leap out after it
as it lurches away under foam
over wing.

A girl is sitting near the wall.
No one has asked her to dance,
tonight or ever.
The couples whirl by, laughing.
She doesn't know what to do with her eyes,
thinks it would be better to be
anywhere else,
thinks it would be better to be dead.
When she knows what to do with her eyes
she'll see that the dancers
are shadows on the wall,
she'll see that the dance was all for her –
her grief.

Don't name your loved one.
Like painted ships in a book the named ones
Sail out of the harbour and flop below the horizon.

Don't name your Beloved
this shimmering flame under the skin
this bird in the hawthorn that answers.

Backwards is the hardest way to go
stony ground, my feet bare.
Turning back from the high, vibrating air,
turning away from the sweet, embracing,
honeysuckle light

and plodding back like a convict
into the valley of damage
again, again.

This tunnel has no ending
and no beginning.
You are not here.
I was following my own shadow.

All the water has drained out of the earth.
I do not know what to do to stop this pain.
You have withdrawn from every grass-blade.
My bones clack together.
A wooden bird hops on the grass.
A stuffed cat watches.
I could slash these veins with a piece of stone.
I do not know how to be in this pain.

When you feel you can't do anything
do the hardest thing.
There's freedom.
Take the Karakorams.
In wartime the soldiers were mad.

In peacetime
dangled new-hatched
pin-head spiders from the cliff-face
dropped their lives like a trail of seeds
engraved inch by inch
through the Karakoram mountains
a highway to China.

And now the crown
to know I can go down
light as a butterfly
into the valley of damage

as Christ descends into pain
arms outstretched
light as a leaf.
You were not gone.
You *are* this grief.

You say you are in control of your life.
Try this:
You are speeding along in a car
at a hundred miles an hour.
Take your hands off the steering wheel
feet off the pedals
close your eyes.

Forgiveness —
what does it mean?
The bodies of the lovers
naked before you
the straight one and the broken
side by side, at rest
as if each slid
from the other's skin.
Hurt unpeeled
wound unsealed
that place inside you
where the stone opens
tears flow from rock.

Never count yourself blessed.
Your loved one is both host and guest.

At first it amused us
the house in the forest, smelling of wild garlic
with no doors, no windows.

We played in its shadow all day.
We pretended:
Pretend it's a castle, a palace, pretend it's ours.

The day became a life.
We saw we were not pretending any more but still
lurked in its shadow

the house that was not a house but somehow a prison
we needed to enter.
We tried to leave, separately, together

but always returned.
At last we unbuttoned our hopes and cast them
among the grasses to seed

we lay down in the weed
at the bottom of the stream, we unfurled our skin
like kites in the wind.

I want the noise to stop.
Telephone in my head.
Motorway in my heart.

I want to lie naked in your love.
To have taken off my body.
To have scrubbed out my name.

This guest, she came to me
from the swamps and slime.
How long have we lain here
locked in this crime
fasting
whispering into the night,
cloistered chaste
as twin white candles, melting
pouring our light out –
this deadly shadow in her
white habit.

Nothing is so real as this.
Our bodies have given up
their title deeds
lie in each other
without boundaries or needs
my heart floating as still and high
as full moon in its bowl of sky.

This is how the universe is made.
He enters her
and love explodes into star
she fine as cell-point
he delicate as pollen
star exploding into flower.